It's a Dog-Gone Good Life

To Angelica,

Enjoy!
Judy Slater
4/08

It's a Dog-Gone Good Life

Poems
by
Judy Slater

Art
by
Florie Freshman

INKWELL PRODUCTIONS®

Published December 2004
by Judy Slater

Printed in the United States of America.

ISBN: 0-9749701-8-2

Library of Congress Control Number: 2004114806

Published by
Inkwell Productions
6962 E. First Avenue, Ste.102
Scottsdale, AZ 85251
Phone (480) 481-6036
Fax (480) 481-6042
Toll Free 888-324-BOOK (2665)
Email: info@inkwellproductions.com
Web site: www.inkwellproductions.com

Dedication

*This collection of poems is dedicated to those loving
creatures that have brightened my life ...
Schultzie, Coco, Tippy, Paco and Pee Jay ...
and to all the canine friends who give their love sweetly,
purely and forever. They do make the human existence so
Dog-Gone Good!*

*I would like to thank Elizabeth Evarts for motivating me
to begin my poetic journey, and for her encouragement
along the way. I am so deeply grateful to the friends
who believed in me even when I couldn't,
especially Cloise Barker, the dearest friend of all.*

YOUR PAGE

My name is _____

My dog's name is _____

Male/Female_____

_____ was born _____

_____ is a (breed) _____

Color _____

_____ is Smart because _____

_____ is Funny because _____

_____ is Unique because _____

I love_____ because _____

Special Tricks_____

_____

Favorite Stories _____

_____

_____

TO BE OR NOT TO BE

Of all the animals in the world
Which one would I like to be
I know if I had my wish
I never would be a fish
All shriveled and wet from the sea

To be a horse chasing flies with my tail
Or getting nowhere so slowly
As a lowly old snail

A fly in fear of a swatter
Or even a cute little otter
Would not be my choice for this tale

I would not be a sheep
'Cause I'd never get sleep
Or a bird whose song is unsung
Or a cow on the "moove"
Watching out for its hooves
Not to step in another cow's dung

I'd tire of playing leapfrog
And never would be a hog
So my first choice would be
The best life I can see
That of my own well-loved dog!

TO BE OR NOT - TWO

Again I am wondering
Who would I like to be
Maybe a Koala bear
Asleep in a tree
No, eating eucalyptus leaves
Is just not for me

How about a baboon
Beating my chest
Well, that stage of evolution
I think I have left

It might be fun to be a gazelle
Gracefully on the run
Or a slow moving tortoise
Basking in the sun

Would I be a coyote
Always on the howl
Or a sneaky old wolf
Forever on the prowl

What's the use of wondering
Whose life is better than the rest
It's the one where you get all the pets,
Of course...A dog's life is surely the best!

TO BE OR NOT - THREE

Watching the animals
Play on TV
I ask once again
Whether I'd like to be...

A giant giraffe
Picking leaves from a tree
High above all others
No, that's too far to see

Hopping around like a cute kangaroo
Would be a big problem for me
I used to enjoy a good game of hopscotch
But that was when I was three

To be the king of the jungle
Is a job I might bungle
And a cool tiger cat
Is not where I'm at

So many choices...
Creatures great and small
But I still believe my dog's life
Is the life that's best of all!

TO BE OR NOT - FOUR

Thoughts of the animals
Who share our space
Come to me again as
I think of the face...

Of a beautiful dolphin
Swimming free in the sea
Now that is one creature
I might like to be

To be smart as an elephant
A thought not to junk
But then I'd need a porter
To carry my trunk

Scurrying non-stop
Like a busy little ant
Working on an assembly line
Imagine that...I can't

I need more stimulation
A life that's fun and good
So it's without hesitation
I choose the life of my dog
(Of course you knew I would!)

TO BE OR NOT - FIVE

Thoughts of the animals
Come into my head
As I sit on my duff
Which sits on my bed...

When suddenly this notion
I couldn't seem to shake
Slithering around the room
I thought I was a snake

Would I really like to be
A rattler or a boa
Feared by man and child alike
A slimy thing...oh, noa

A big black bear
Asleep behind a tree
Hibernating for months right there
Doesn't sound like fun to me

Constantly clucking like a chicken
Full of eggs to lay
My full belly would make me sicken
So I'll have to say...nay, nay

Back to the beginning
Where I still can see the light
My doggie's life's the best of all
The one for which I'd fight!

TO BE OR NOT - SIX

Watching the hummingbirds drinking
Started me to thinking
What a life it must be
To be a bird and fly free
But all that flapping around
Would surely tire me

Could I be a chimpanzee
Sitting atop the limb of a tree
Beating my chest and picking off lice
For them, it's ok
For me, not so nice

Might I be a moose
With big antlers on my head
Could I carry them around
Without their coming loose

Or a calico cat purring content
Free to eat atop the counter
And never pay a cent of rent
Or a mouse on the run
From the cat's speedy chase
My bet's on the cat to conquer this race

Whatever bet you make
The answer's still the same
My doggie is the winner
In this cat and mouse game!

TO BE OR NOT - SEVEN

When the temperature is hot
And the summer days are lazy
If I had to wear the shell of an armadillo
I surely would go crazy

Looking for a cool place to hide
I might be a lizard
Slithering around the desert
Hoping (ha, ha) for a blizzard

Still trying hard to cool off
I felt a breeze pass by
But, alas, it was just a moth
Or was it a dragon fly

If I was an iguana
I'd like the desert heat
I'd do just what I wanna
And never need a seat

How silly can I be
Why do I even ponder
My doggie lives in air-conditioned splendor
And has no need to wander!

TO BE OR NOT - EIGHT

If I lived in Australia
I might be a doggie dingo
Running around the Outback
Trying to learn the lingo

I'm not sheepish like a ewe
Or as funny looking as an emu
I can't honk like a donkey
Or climb like a monkey
So here's what I say to you...

If you want a life of leisure
Choose the one with all the pleasure
Kisses, hugs, and lots of pets
A doggie's life's as good as it gets!

TO BE OR NOT - NINE

A hippopotamus in need of a diet
Or a scary crocodile causing a riot
Is not what I'd like to be

I don't want to be a tubby
Or feared or flabby or flubby
Can you really blame me?

An ancient scaly dragon
Spiting fire all the day
I'd drink so much water to quench
My thirst I might just float away

So here I sit watching his highness
Lounging on my bed
Enjoying life to the fullest
What could be better, he said!

TO BE OR NOT - TEN

If I were a porcupine
Everyone would fear my prickles
Nobody would think I'm fine
They'd know to touch me would not tickle

They might take me for a pineapple
And bite me like I was an apple
Oh, my, with a mouthful of prickles
They would be oh so sickles

No, I would not be a porcupine
I want people near me
Not to fear me
Just like that precious doggie of mine!

TO BE OR NOT - ELEVEN

As I listen to the slurping sound
Of my little doggie drinking
I can't help but start to thinking...

Would I be a unicorn
A unique animal at that
But with a horn upon my head
How would I wear my favorite hat

I wouldn't be a yucky rodent
Circling through a maze
Looking for the right way out
It's not the way I'd spend my days

And if I was a rooster
I'd put my neighbors in a stew
'Cause every morning they'd be wakened
By my "cock-a-doodle-doo"

No stew, no maze, no horns upon my head
There is no question in my mind
The sweet life of a dog
Is the one I'll take instead!

TO BE OR NOT - TWELVE

There he lies upon the floor
His head upon his little paw
Looking content and oh so comfy
How could I ever want to be...

A panther or a puma
On the chase to catch their prey
I'd rather catch a can of tuna
It's much easier, any day

A whale is a mammal
Just like me
Among the smartest of all animals
But he lives beneath the sea
No bed, no blanket to keep him warm
Only blubber (which is fat, you know)
To help him weather any storm
He never has to diet
Or eat low-cal cuisine
His great size gives him so much might
He doesn't have to prove he's mean
Although his enemies are few
I still don't want him on my bed
Do you

I want to be loved and cuddled and adored
And welcomed with open arms
Who could resist a puppy's face
And all his many charms?

TO BE OR NOT - THIRTEEN

When the holidays come 'round
I might like to be a reindeer
Pulling Santa's sleigh with cheer
Guiding him without a sound

But then an owl makes a noise
"Hoot, hoot" awakening the girls and boys
Putting fear into the night
Causing antlers to shake with fright

No, I won't be a reindeer pulling a sleigh
It's the very hard work I'd dread
For my doggie, each day is a holiday
And his only job is finding his bed!

TO BE OR NOT - FOURTEEN

If I was a zebra
With stripes all over me
People might think I was a prisoner
Running from the law, you see

Then, again, if I was a skunk
Nobody would get close
They'd say I stunk
And hold their nose
And run from me in droves

I must admit there are some times
When doggies don't smell good
They roll in dirt and need a bath
Which they would take...if they could
But then they cock their heads to say
"So, I'm smelly...
but I'm cute and lovable anyway!"

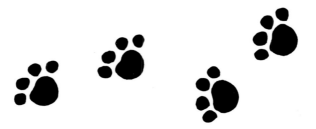

TO BE OR NOT - FIFTEEN

To be a cute little bunny
With great big ears a-flopping
Eating my way through vegetation
Plopping without hardly stopping

Or a jackrabbit hiding in a bush
Running so fast, always in a rush
No time has he
For a good hearty lunch

If I liked to eat a nut
A squirrel I might be
But that would put me in a rut
I would not have variety

My dog has meals served to him
He doesn't have to scavenge
His situation is win-win
Making him a beast not savage!

TO BE OR NOT - SIXTEEN

If I lived in the ocean
I could be in perpetual motion...

With eight arms flailing
Like a squid
Avoiding bigger fish
Would be all I did

Or a fearful, preying shark
With teeth so big and powerful jaw
I'd never want for food to gnaw
But, like a dog, I couldn't bark

Swimming upstream
In fear of a net
A salmon I might be
I'd be caught for someone's dinner
Then there would be
No more me

How about a big old seal
Sunning on a rock
Fins a flapping
Honking and yapping
This does have some appeal

Comfort is my goal
And dry land more my style
In comparison to all others
It's a dog-gone good life
All the while!

TO BE OR NOT - SEVENTEEN

If I wore a tuxedo
I might be a penguin looking for a date
I'd strut around until I found
A pretty gal to be my mate

We'd celebrate with turkey dinner
Formal, of course, you see
But being a turkey's sure not a winner
"Cause it would be the death of me

We'd invite our friend the three-toed sloth
If we could get him out of the tree
Where he hangs around all day long
And is lazy and slow as can be

My doggie needs no clothes to wear
He comes and goes in the rough
No costly bills for him to bear
What a life...mine should be so tough!

TO BE OR NOT - EIGHTEEN

Looking up at a clear blue sky
I see a bald eagle soar
So graceful and gallant is he
Such a rare sight to see
Why, I ask, aren't there more

Magnificent manatees
Powerful blue whales
Mammals just like us
Bighorn sheep and other species
Disappearing with little fuss

Orangutans and grizzly bears
Also on the list
So is the panda
Who comes from China
They'd all be sorely missed

The condor and the whooping crane
Endangered creatures, too
Did not we humans foresee the pain
Of a world that exists just for the gain
Of a greedy and careless few

There but for fortune goes the life
Of a dog, loved unconditionally
And protected from strife
Living with humans and others alike
In peace and harmony
With no need to fight

HE'S COOL

Here's a clue for all of you...
If you're hot and need some air
Don't sit before the fridgidaire
And if you're looking for some cool
No need to jump into the pool
Do you crave that comfort zone
A place to curl up in your home
I'll tell you what to do...

Just look for the place
Your doggie has found
It's surely the coolest,
Most comfortable around!

FOR PACO & PEE JAY

I love you when you're dirty
I love you when you're clean
I love you when you're sweet as sugar
I love you 'cause you're never mean

I love you in the morning
When I awake to see your face
Throughout the day and in the night
When on my bed you take your place

I love you when you're feisty
I love you when you're bold
I love you more and more each day
Because I fear you're growing old

I love you now and will tomorrow
And for eternity
For when we part I know this love
Will always be with me

TELLTALE TAIL

A doggie's tail is a telltale tail
A tale of joy
A tale of woe
A tale of fear
When it hangs so low

A challenging tail
High in the air
Ready to fight
If another dog dares

A tale of sick
A tale of well
Wagging its feelings
His story to tell

Tales of all kinds
Are told by the tails
Of the doggie's who wear them
On their little behinds

SLEEPING DOGS

Sometimes they sleep on their sides
Sometimes on their backs or tummies
No doubt dreaming of the tricks
They might do to get a yummy

No shame have they
With legs outstretched
Revealing all their manly parts
(Not the ones they use to fetch)

Ah, what a life to be a dog
Who will always sleep so well
They will never have the need
To take a sleeping pill!

FOR THE LOVE OF A PET

The love we share is true and pure
Constant and never changing
From day to day it stays that way
It feels so good, so sure

Our little furry friends
Let us be who we are
They show us how to love up close
Not like humans
Who may stay afar

A piece of our hearts forever theirs
Our lives eternally entwined
They ask so little and give so much
They can make a lesser man kind

And when it's time for them to go
The memory of their loving grace
Will fill the space
Until their face
We will again shall know

EYELASHES TO DIE FOR

Ears that flop in the breeze
A tushie that plops where it pleases
A brown button nose that glistens
Whenever he sneezes

Better than a maid
Cleaning crumbs from my floor
He barks so I'm not afraid
When strangers come to the door

Eyelashes to die for
A sweetness to cry for
Fur so soft to the touch
My Paco, I love you so much

THE DOG WHO WOULD BE KING

There was a pet dog who was king
He thought he was King of EVERYTHING

Of dogs and cats
And boys and girls
Of EVERYTHING
In all the world

Of lions and tigers
And lazy old llamas
Of EVERYTHING
Including his mama

What made this little dog feel so above
It must be because he was gifted with love

THE GREATEST GIFT

A greater grief I've hardly known
Than losing a friend who shared
My home, my joys and my pain
Always there, in sun and rain
Your ever-loving face so close
When I needed comfort most
I'll miss the tinkling of your tags
The patter of your little feet
Your kisses on my sleeping face
Your joyous tail across my cheek
Silence rests in lonely rooms
Time without you skips a beat
A greater gift I'll never give
Than loving you as I did

THE PRINCE

There is a little cockapoo named Pee Jay
Who became a Prince from the first day
As the runt of the litter
He was treated much better
And was never aware of another way

His father was Paco, the King
Who gave him just about everything
The food from his dish
And many a kiss
He wanted not for a thing

Playing with Paco was fun
It kept his father young
He loved to tease him
Not so much to please him
It was funny to see Paco run

The Prince and the King were inseparable
The love they shared immeasurable
Yet Pee Jay knew from the start
Paco was first in my heart
And that was just not acceptable

So the cute little imp did some "shouldn'ts"
To get my attention he wouldn't
Mind squatting inside
Unafraid of the chide
Thinking his mother just couldn't

Then the fateful day came, alas
When the King's kingdom finally did pass
At first lonely and sad
Pee Jay realized he had
All his mother's attention at last

Now, as Pee Jay gets older and older
The depth of our love seems bolder
He needs me so much
His soft fur I touch
The thought of our parting grows colder

Without sight in one eye and hearing impaired
He still sometimes acts like a young one
Though older than fifteen the doc said he's spared
The aging effects that will come

So together we enjoy the time left
Until fate's unkindly hand
Makes me once again bereft

HEAVEN

If heaven is a place
To go after this life is through
I think that I would like to know
That I could have it
Just like you

My new life would always be
So sweet and so carefree
I'd play
And sleep
And play
And eat

I'd have my very own butler and maid
And they would wait on me
Hand and feet
And if I performed some silly trick
They'd offer me a yummy treat

I'd never want for pets
Or back and belly rubs
Tons of kisses I would get
I'd know how much I was loved

Oh what a life it would be
For, after all, god spelled backwards
Happens to be DOG!

GLOSSARY OF BREEDS

COVER - Cockapoo (Paco)

MEDICAL HISTORY

VACCINATIONS

	Month	Day	Year

Rabies
(every 3 years)

Distemper / Parvo
(annual)

Corona Virus
(annual)

Bordetella /
Canine Cough
(annual)

Other

MEDICAL HISTORY

DOCTOR VISITS

	Month	Day	Year

Check Ups:

_____

_____

_____

_____

_____

_____

_____

Other

_____

_____

_____

_____

ABOUT THE AUTHOR - JUDY SLATER

Born in New York City, Judy moved to Phoenix, Arizona, in 1976, with one dog, one husband and some personal belongings, never dreaming that one day she would become an author. After graduating from colllege with a BA in Psychology, she worked for CBS-TV, Cooper Union College of Art & Architecture, in Real Estate, Social Service, and finally, for the past 17 years, as a Promotional Products and Marketing consultant.

Judy's first dog, a little cream-colored toy poodle named Coco, was a surprise gift for her eighth birthday. This was the beginning of a deeply felt love relationship with all the pooches who have shared her life since. The music that is written from the bond between a dog and his human companion, for Judy, is comparable to no other. It is a beautiful composition that has eased the physical and other challenges she has faced these many years.

If you have a story, anecdote, or words you would like to share about this book, please send them to *It's A Dog-Gone Good Life*, c/o Inkwell Productions, 6962 East First Avenue, Suite 102, Scottsdale, Arizona 85251.

ABOUT THE ARTIST -
FLORIE FRESHMAN

Florie Freshman spent childhood summers on the Seagate Beach
and in the mountains of New York. A caricaturist, actress, singer,
dancer, writer, composer and Tarot card reader, Florie has
illustrated several children's books for Waldman Publishing in
New York City. Her first writing venture,
Uncle Hershel Overmine Shoulder, is filled with cartoons and
comes with a CD of original music which she sings.
It is being published by Inkwell Productions.

She dedicates this poem to her cat, Rusty Iron Topaz Oodidah,
who felt all cats have a right to keep their 18 claws intact:

They don't run up to lick your nose,
Cats just sit and dramatically pose,
They coze and doze without foes nor woes,
I'd be a cat if I could've chose.

Florie would like to thank her sister, Lee Kaster, for helping
with layout and computer graphics, to Dixie for finding reference
material, and to Daddy and Malka for their free advice.
Special thanks to Lisa, Regina and Hershel up in Heaven.